You have done something truly amazing! You committed to a life in recovery from addiction!

Maybe you've been in recovery for [...] your journey. Regardless of where [...] practicing daily gratitude can help [...]

Gratitude reinforces the positive things you have in your life rather than focusing on what you are lacking. Showing gratitude helps foster calmness and a peaceful feeling of acceptance. Gratitude brings a feeling of happiness. Gratitude helps to ground, center, and be in the present moment.

This journal is designed to not only give you a place to record your daily gratitude, but also record your daily positive affirmations.

Affirmations help to retrain your brain to focus on positive change and support you through your recovery.

Affirmations are statements such as "I am clean and sober", "I am enough", or "I am strong". Affirmations start with the phrase "I am" because that brings you into the mindset that you have already achieved. These statements retrain your mind to believe, and what you believe, you will receive!

Track a full year of days sober and your mood on the daily trackers as reinforcement of the progress you are making. The month is left blank for you to fill in so you can start your grateful journey anytime in the year. Define a color for each mood on the legend, then color each day's block to reflect your mood for that day.

Sobriety Tracker

1									
2									
3									
4									
5									
6									
7									
8									
9									
10									
11									
12									
13									
14									
15									
16									
17									
18									
19									
20									
21									
22									
23									
24									
25									
26									
27									
28									
29									
30									
31									

Mood Tracker

1
2
3
4
5
6
7
8
9
10
11
12
13
14
15
16
17
18
19
20
21
22
23
24
25
26
27
28
29
30
31

Date: 5/02/24

Today I Am Grateful For: the cinema and relaxing and allowing myself to enjoy life

Todays Affirmation: I am okay the way I am. I do not need fixing.

Date: _____

Today I Am Grateful For:

Todays Affirmation:

Date: _____

Today I Am Grateful For:

Todays Affirmation:

Date: _____

Today I Am Grateful For:

Todays Affirmation:

I am thankful For
Never Giving Up

Date: _____

Today I Am Grateful For:

Todays Affirmation:

Date: _____

Today I Am Grateful For:

Todays Affirmation:

Date: _____

Today I Am Grateful For:

Todays Affirmation:

Date: _____

Today I Am Grateful For:

Todays Affirmation:

Date: _____

Today I Am Grateful For:

Todays Affirmation:

Date: _____

Today I Am Grateful For:

Todays Affirmation:

Date: _____

Today I Am Grateful For:

Todays Affirmation:

Today is a Beautiful Day

Date: _____

Today I Am Grateful For:

Todays Affirmation:

Date: _____

Today I Am Grateful For:

Todays Affirmation:

Date: _____

Today I Am Grateful For:

Todays Affirmation:

Date: _____

Today I Am Grateful For:

Todays Affirmation:

Date: _____

Today I Am Grateful For:

Todays Affirmation:

Date: _____

Today I Am Grateful For:

Todays Affirmation:

Date: _____

Today I Am Grateful For:

Todays Affirmation:

I ACCEPT AND LOVE MYSELF

Date: _____

Today I Am Grateful For:

Todays Affirmation:

Date: _____

Today I Am Grateful For:

Todays Affirmation:

Date: _____

Today I Am Grateful For:

Todays Affirmation:

Date: _____

Today I Am Grateful For:

Todays Affirmation:

Date: _____

Today I Am Grateful For:

Todays Affirmation:

Date: _____

Today I Am Grateful For:

Todays Affirmation:

Date: _____

Today I Am Grateful For:

Todays Affirmation:

I AM STRONGER THAN I KNOW

Date: _____

Today I Am Grateful For:

Todays Affirmation:

Date: _____

Today I Am Grateful For:

Todays Affirmation:

Date: _____

Today I Am Grateful For:

Todays Affirmation:

Date: _____

Today I Am Grateful For:

Todays Affirmation:

Date: _____

Today I Am Grateful For:

Todays Affirmation:

Date: _____

Today I Am Grateful For:

Todays Affirmation:

Date: _____

Today I Am Grateful For:

Todays Affirmation:

Every day is a step forward

Date: _____

Today I Am Grateful For:

Todays Affirmation:

Date: _____

Today I Am Grateful For:

Todays Affirmation:

Date: _____

Today I Am Grateful For:

Todays Affirmation:

Date: _____

Today I Am Grateful For:

Todays Affirmation:

Date: _____

Today I Am Grateful For:

Todays Affirmation:

Date: _____

Today I Am Grateful For:

Todays Affirmation:

Date: _____

Today I Am Grateful For:

Todays Affirmation:

Focus on right now

Date: _____

Today I Am Grateful For:

Todays Affirmation:

Date: _____

Today I Am Grateful For:

Todays Affirmation:

Date: _____

Today I Am Grateful For:

Todays Affirmation:

Date: _____

Today I Am Grateful For:

Todays Affirmation:

Date: _____

Today I Am Grateful For:

Todays Affirmation:

Date: _____

Today I Am Grateful For:

Todays Affirmation:

Date: _____

Today I Am Grateful For:

Todays Affirmation:

You are loved

Date: _____

Today I Am Grateful For:

Todays Affirmation:

Date: _____

Today I Am Grateful For:

Todays Affirmation:

Date: _____

Today I Am Grateful For:

Todays Affirmation:

Date: _____

Today I Am Grateful For:

Todays Affirmation:

Date: _____

Today I Am Grateful For:

Todays Affirmation:

Date: _____

Today I Am Grateful For:

Todays Affirmation:

Date: _____

Today I Am Grateful For:

Todays Affirmation:

Today is an opportunity

Date: _____

Today I Am Grateful For:

Todays Affirmation:

Date: _____

Today I Am Grateful For:

Todays Affirmation:

Date: _____

Today I Am Grateful For:

Todays Affirmation:

Date: _____

Today I Am Grateful For:

Todays Affirmation:

Date: _____

Today I Am Grateful For:

Todays Affirmation:

Date: _____

Today I Am Grateful For:

Todays Affirmation:

Date: _____

Today I Am Grateful For:

Todays Affirmation:

Old ways won't open new doors

Date: _____

Today I Am Grateful For:

Todays Affirmation:

Date: _____

Today I Am Grateful For:

Todays Affirmation:

Date: _____

Today I Am Grateful For:

Todays Affirmation:

Date: _____

Today I Am Grateful For:

Todays Affirmation:

Date: _____

Today I Am Grateful For:

Todays Affirmation:

Date: _____

Today I Am Grateful For:

Todays Affirmation:

Date: _____

Today I Am Grateful For:

Todays Affirmation:

You've got this

Date: _____

Today I Am Grateful For:

Todays Affirmation:

Date: _____

Today I Am Grateful For:

Todays Affirmation:

Date: _____

Today I Am Grateful For:

Todays Affirmation:

Date: _____

Today I Am Grateful For:

Todays Affirmation:

Date: _____

Today I Am Grateful For:

Todays Affirmation:

Date: _____

Today I Am Grateful For:

Todays Affirmation:

Date: _____

Today I Am Grateful For:

Todays Affirmation:

Positivity is a choice

Date: _____

Today I Am Grateful For:

Todays Affirmation:

Date: _____

Today I Am Grateful For:

Todays Affirmation:

Date: _____

Today I Am Grateful For:

Todays Affirmation:

Date: _____

Today I Am Grateful For:

Todays Affirmation:

Date: _____

Today I Am Grateful For:

Todays Affirmation:

Date: _____

Today I Am Grateful For:

Todays Affirmation:

Date: _____

Today I Am Grateful For:

Todays Affirmation:

You are free to fly

Date: _____

Today I Am Grateful For:

Todays Affirmation:

Date: _____

Today I Am Grateful For:

Todays Affirmation:

Date: _____

Today I Am Grateful For:

Todays Affirmation:

Date: _____

Today I Am Grateful For:

Todays Affirmation:

Date: _____

Today I Am Grateful For:

Todays Affirmation:

Date: _____

Today I Am Grateful For:

Todays Affirmation:

Date: _____

Today I Am Grateful For:

Todays Affirmation:

Life is tough but so are you

Date: _____

Today I Am Grateful For:

Todays Affirmation:

Date: _____

Today I Am Grateful For:

Todays Affirmation:

Date: _____

Today I Am Grateful For:

Todays Affirmation:

Date: _____

Today I Am Grateful For:

Todays Affirmation:

Date: _____

Today I Am Grateful For:

Todays Affirmation:

Date: _____

Today I Am Grateful For:

Todays Affirmation:

Date: _____

Today I Am Grateful For:

Todays Affirmation:

You don't have to be perfect
To be amazing

Date: _____

Today I Am Grateful For:

Todays Affirmation:

Date: _____

Today I Am Grateful For:

Todays Affirmation:

Date: _____

Today I Am Grateful For:

Todays Affirmation:

Date: _____

Today I Am Grateful For:

Todays Affirmation:

Date: _____

Today I Am Grateful For:

Todays Affirmation:

Date: _____

Today I Am Grateful For:

Todays Affirmation:

Date: _____

Today I Am Grateful For:

Todays Affirmation:

Be stronger than Your excuses

Date: _____

Today I Am Grateful For:

Todays Affirmation:

Date: _____

Today I Am Grateful For:

Todays Affirmation:

Date: _____

Today I Am Grateful For:

Todays Affirmation:

Date: _____

Today I Am Grateful For:

Todays Affirmation:

Date: _____

Today I Am Grateful For:

Todays Affirmation:

Date: _____

Today I Am Grateful For:

Todays Affirmation:

Date: _____

Today I Am Grateful For:

Todays Affirmation:

I AM ENOUGH

Date: _____

Today I Am Grateful For:

Todays Affirmation:

Date: _____

Today I Am Grateful For:

Todays Affirmation:

Date: _____

Today I Am Grateful For:

Todays Affirmation:

Date: _____

Today I Am Grateful For:

Todays Affirmation:

Date: _____

Today I Am Grateful For:

Todays Affirmation:

Date: _____

Today I Am Grateful For:

Todays Affirmation:

Date: _____

Today I Am Grateful For:

Todays Affirmation:

Happiness is not a destination

Date: _____

Today I Am Grateful For:

Todays Affirmation:

Date: _____

Today I Am Grateful For:

Todays Affirmation:

Date: _____

Today I Am Grateful For:

Todays Affirmation:

Date: _____

Today I Am Grateful For:

Todays Affirmation:

Date: _____

Today I Am Grateful For:

Todays Affirmation:

Date: _____

Today I Am Grateful For:

Todays Affirmation:

Date: _____

Today I Am Grateful For:

Todays Affirmation:

You don't grow when you're comfortable

Date: _____

Today I Am Grateful For:

Todays Affirmation:

Date: _____

Today I Am Grateful For:

Todays Affirmation:

Date: _____

Today I Am Grateful For:

Todays Affirmation:

Date: _____

Today I Am Grateful For:

Todays Affirmation:

Date: _____

Today I Am Grateful For:

Todays Affirmation:

Date: _____

Today I Am Grateful For:

Todays Affirmation:

Date: _____

Today I Am Grateful For:

Todays Affirmation:

Believe in yourself

Date: _____

Today I Am Grateful For:

Todays Affirmation:

Date: _____

Today I Am Grateful For:

Todays Affirmation:

Date: _____

Today I Am Grateful For:

Todays Affirmation:

Date: _____

Today I Am Grateful For:

Todays Affirmation:

Date: _____

Today I Am Grateful For:

Todays Affirmation:

Date: _____

Today I Am Grateful For:

Todays Affirmation:

Date: _____

Today I Am Grateful For:

Todays Affirmation:

Sometimes it's ok if the only thing you did today was breathe

---

Date: _____

Today I Am Grateful For:

Todays Affirmation:

Date: _____

Today I Am Grateful For:

Todays Affirmation:

Date: _____

Today I Am Grateful For:

Todays Affirmation:

Date: _____

Today I Am Grateful For:

Todays Affirmation:

Date: _____

Today I Am Grateful For:

Todays Affirmation:

Date: _____

Today I Am Grateful For:

Todays Affirmation:

Date: _____

Today I Am Grateful For:

Todays Affirmation:

Let go of what you can't control

Date: _____

Today I Am Grateful For:

Todays Affirmation:

Date: _____

Today I Am Grateful For:

Todays Affirmation:

Date: _____

Today I Am Grateful For:

Todays Affirmation:

Date: _____
Today I Am Grateful For:
Todays Affirmation:

Date: _____
Today I Am Grateful For:
Todays Affirmation:

Date: _____
Today I Am Grateful For:
Todays Affirmation:

Date: _____
Today I Am Grateful For:
Todays Affirmation:

You are a warrior

Date: _____

Today I Am Grateful For:

Todays Affirmation:

Date: _____

Today I Am Grateful For:

Todays Affirmation:

Date: _____

Today I Am Grateful For:

Todays Affirmation:

Date: _____

Today I Am Grateful For:

Todays Affirmation:

Date: _____

Today I Am Grateful For:

Todays Affirmation:

Date: _____

Today I Am Grateful For:

Todays Affirmation:

Date: _____

Today I Am Grateful For:

Todays Affirmation:

It's a good day to be happy

Date: _____

Today I Am Grateful For:

Todays Affirmation:

Date: _____

Today I Am Grateful For:

Todays Affirmation:

Date: _____

Today I Am Grateful For:

Todays Affirmation:

Date: _____

Today I Am Grateful For:

Todays Affirmation:

Date: _____

Today I Am Grateful For:

Todays Affirmation:

Date: _____

Today I Am Grateful For:

Todays Affirmation:

Date: _____

Today I Am Grateful For:

Todays Affirmation:

Don't look back
You're not going that way

Date: _____

Today I Am Grateful For:

Todays Affirmation:

Date: _____

Today I Am Grateful For:

Todays Affirmation:

Date: _____

Today I Am Grateful For:

Todays Affirmation:

Date: _____

Today I Am Grateful For:

Todays Affirmation:

Date: _____

Today I Am Grateful For:

Todays Affirmation:

Date: _____

Today I Am Grateful For:

Todays Affirmation:

Date: _____

Today I Am Grateful For:

Todays Affirmation:

If it doesn't challenge you it won't change you

Date: _____

Today I Am Grateful For:

Todays Affirmation:

Date: _____

Today I Am Grateful For:

Todays Affirmation:

Date: _____

Today I Am Grateful For:

Todays Affirmation:

Date: _____

Today I Am Grateful For:

Todays Affirmation:

Date: _____

Today I Am Grateful For:

Todays Affirmation:

Date: _____

Today I Am Grateful For:

Todays Affirmation:

Date: _____

Today I Am Grateful For:

Todays Affirmation:

Be awesome today

Date: _____

Today I Am Grateful For:

Todays Affirmation:

Date: _____

Today I Am Grateful For:

Todays Affirmation:

Date: _____

Today I Am Grateful For:

Todays Affirmation:

Date: _____

Today I Am Grateful For:

Todays Affirmation:

Date: _____

Today I Am Grateful For:

Todays Affirmation:

Date: _____

Today I Am Grateful For:

Todays Affirmation:

Date: _____

Today I Am Grateful For:

Todays Affirmation:

Keep going
Don't quit

Date: _____

Today I Am Grateful For:

Todays Affirmation:

Date: _____

Today I Am Grateful For:

Todays Affirmation:

Date: _____

Today I Am Grateful For:

Todays Affirmation:

Date: _____

Today I Am Grateful For:

Todays Affirmation:

Date: _____

Today I Am Grateful For:

Todays Affirmation:

Date: _____

Today I Am Grateful For:

Todays Affirmation:

Date: _____

Today I Am Grateful For:

Todays Affirmation:

I'm not what happened to me
I am what I choose to become

Date: _____

Today I Am Grateful For:

Todays Affirmation:

Date: _____

Today I Am Grateful For:

Todays Affirmation:

Date: _____

Today I Am Grateful For:

Todays Affirmation:

Date: _____

Today I Am Grateful For:

Todays Affirmation:

Date: _____

Today I Am Grateful For:

Todays Affirmation:

Date: _____

Today I Am Grateful For:

Todays Affirmation:

Date: _____

Today I Am Grateful For:

Todays Affirmation:

Make your reasons better than your excuses

Date: _____

Today I Am Grateful For:

Todays Affirmation:

Date: _____

Today I Am Grateful For:

Todays Affirmation:

Date: _____

Today I Am Grateful For:

Todays Affirmation:

Date: _____

Today I Am Grateful For:

Todays Affirmation:

Date: _____

Today I Am Grateful For:

Todays Affirmation:

Date: _____

Today I Am Grateful For:

Todays Affirmation:

Date: _____

Today I Am Grateful For:

Todays Affirmation:

Dear life, I love you

Date: _____

Today I Am Grateful For:

Todays Affirmation:

Date: _____

Today I Am Grateful For:

Todays Affirmation:

Date: _____

Today I Am Grateful For:

Todays Affirmation:

Date: _____

Today I Am Grateful For:

Todays Affirmation:

Date: _____

Today I Am Grateful For:

Todays Affirmation:

Date: _____

Today I Am Grateful For:

Todays Affirmation:

Date: _____

Today I Am Grateful For:

Todays Affirmation:

Be your own hero

Date: _____

Today I Am Grateful For:

Todays Affirmation:

Date: _____

Today I Am Grateful For:

Todays Affirmation:

Date: _____

Today I Am Grateful For:

Todays Affirmation:

Date: _____

Today I Am Grateful For:

Todays Affirmation:

Date: _____

Today I Am Grateful For:

Todays Affirmation:

Date: _____

Today I Am Grateful For:

Todays Affirmation:

Date: _____

Today I Am Grateful For:

Todays Affirmation:

Everything's gonna be alright

Date: _____

Today I Am Grateful For:

Todays Affirmation:

Date: _____

Today I Am Grateful For:

Todays Affirmation:

Date: _____

Today I Am Grateful For:

Todays Affirmation:

Date: _____

Today I Am Grateful For:

Todays Affirmation:

Date: _____

Today I Am Grateful For:

Todays Affirmation:

Date: _____

Today I Am Grateful For:

Todays Affirmation:

Date: _____

Today I Am Grateful For:

Todays Affirmation:

Yesterday is history
tomorrow is a mystery

Date: _____

Today I Am Grateful For:

Todays Affirmation:

Date: _____

Today I Am Grateful For:

Todays Affirmation:

Date: _____

Today I Am Grateful For:

Todays Affirmation:

Date: _____

Today I Am Grateful For:

Todays Affirmation:

Date: _____

Today I Am Grateful For:

Todays Affirmation:

Date: _____

Today I Am Grateful For:

Todays Affirmation:

Date: _____

Today I Am Grateful For:

Todays Affirmation:

Strive for progress not perfection

Date: _____

Today I Am Grateful For:

Todays Affirmation:

Date: _____

Today I Am Grateful For:

Todays Affirmation:

Date: _____

Today I Am Grateful For:

Todays Affirmation:

Date: _____

Today I Am Grateful For:

Todays Affirmation:

Date: _____

Today I Am Grateful For:

Todays Affirmation:

Date: _____

Today I Am Grateful For:

Todays Affirmation:

Date: _____

Today I Am Grateful For:

Todays Affirmation:

Each morning we are born again

Date: _____

Today I Am Grateful For:

Todays Affirmation:

Date: _____

Today I Am Grateful For:

Todays Affirmation:

Date: _____

Today I Am Grateful For:

Todays Affirmation:

Date: _____

Today I Am Grateful For:

Todays Affirmation:

Date: _____

Today I Am Grateful For:

Todays Affirmation:

Date: _____

Today I Am Grateful For:

Todays Affirmation:

Date: _____

Today I Am Grateful For:

Todays Affirmation:

Believe you can and you're halfway there

Date: _____

Today I Am Grateful For:

Todays Affirmation:

Date: _____

Today I Am Grateful For:

Todays Affirmation:

Date: _____

Today I Am Grateful For:

Todays Affirmation:

Date: _____

Today I Am Grateful For:

Todays Affirmation:

Date: _____

Today I Am Grateful For:

Todays Affirmation:

Date: _____

Today I Am Grateful For:

Todays Affirmation:

Date: _____

Today I Am Grateful For:

Todays Affirmation:

Do all things with love

Date: _____

Today I Am Grateful For:

Todays Affirmation:

Date: _____

Today I Am Grateful For:

Todays Affirmation:

Date: _____

Today I Am Grateful For:

Todays Affirmation:

Date: _____

Today I Am Grateful For:

Todays Affirmation:

Date: _____

Today I Am Grateful For:

Todays Affirmation:

Date: _____

Today I Am Grateful For:

Todays Affirmation:

Date: _____

Today I Am Grateful For:

Todays Affirmation:

My only competition is who I was yesterday

Date: _____

Today I Am Grateful For:

Todays Affirmation:

Date: _____

Today I Am Grateful For:

Todays Affirmation:

Date: _____

Today I Am Grateful For:

Todays Affirmation:

Date: _____

Today I Am Grateful For:

Todays Affirmation:

Date: _____

Today I Am Grateful For:

Todays Affirmation:

Date: _____

Today I Am Grateful For:

Todays Affirmation:

Date: _____

Today I Am Grateful For:

Todays Affirmation:

Trust the process

Date: _____

Today I Am Grateful For:

Todays Affirmation:

Date: _____

Today I Am Grateful For:

Todays Affirmation:

Date: _____

Today I Am Grateful For:

Todays Affirmation:

Date: _____

Today I Am Grateful For:

Todays Affirmation:

Date: _____

Today I Am Grateful For:

Todays Affirmation:

Date: _____

Today I Am Grateful For:

Todays Affirmation:

Date: _____

Today I Am Grateful For:

Todays Affirmation:

You can do anything but not everything

Date: _____

Today I Am Grateful For:

Todays Affirmation:

Date: _____

Today I Am Grateful For:

Todays Affirmation:

Date: _____

Today I Am Grateful For:

Todays Affirmation:

Date: _____

Today I Am Grateful For:

Todays Affirmation:

Date: _____

Today I Am Grateful For:

Todays Affirmation:

Date: _____

Today I Am Grateful For:

Todays Affirmation:

Date: _____

Today I Am Grateful For:

Todays Affirmation:

Do something that your future self will thank you for

Date: _____

Today I Am Grateful For:

Todays Affirmation:

Date: _____

Today I Am Grateful For:

Todays Affirmation:

Date: _____

Today I Am Grateful For:

Todays Affirmation:

Date: _____

Today I Am Grateful For:

Todays Affirmation:

Date: _____

Today I Am Grateful For:

Todays Affirmation:

Date: _____

Today I Am Grateful For:

Todays Affirmation:

Date: _____

Today I Am Grateful For:

Todays Affirmation:

The best is yet to come

Date: _____

Today I Am Grateful For:

Todays Affirmation:

Date: _____

Today I Am Grateful For:

Todays Affirmation:

Date: _____

Today I Am Grateful For:

Todays Affirmation:

Date: _____

Today I Am Grateful For:

Todays Affirmation:

Date: _____

Today I Am Grateful For:

Todays Affirmation:

Date: _____

Today I Am Grateful For:

Todays Affirmation:

Date: _____

Today I Am Grateful For:

Todays Affirmation:

Today I will not stress over things I can't control

Date: _____

Today I Am Grateful For:

Todays Affirmation:

Date: _____

Today I Am Grateful For:

Todays Affirmation:

Date: _____

Today I Am Grateful For:

Todays Affirmation:

Date: _____

Today I Am Grateful For:

Todays Affirmation:

Date: _____

Today I Am Grateful For:

Todays Affirmation:

Date: _____

Today I Am Grateful For:

Todays Affirmation:

Date: _____

Today I Am Grateful For:

Todays Affirmation:

Every day may not be good
But there is something good
In every day

Date: _____

Today I Am Grateful For:

Todays Affirmation:

Date: _____

Today I Am Grateful For:

Todays Affirmation:

Date: _____

Today I Am Grateful For:

Todays Affirmation:

DATE: _____

Today I Am Grateful For:

Todays Affirmation:

DATE: _____

Today I Am Grateful For:

Todays Affirmation:

DATE: _____

Today I Am Grateful For:

Todays Affirmation:

DATE: _____

Today I Am Grateful For:

Todays Affirmation:

You've been assigned this mountain
To show others it can be moved

Date: _____

Today I Am Grateful For:

Todays Affirmation:

Date: _____

Today I Am Grateful For:

Todays Affirmation:

Date: _____

Today I Am Grateful For:

Todays Affirmation:

Date: _____

Today I Am Grateful For:

Todays Affirmation:

Date: _____

Today I Am Grateful For:

Todays Affirmation:

Date: _____

Today I Am Grateful For:

Todays Affirmation:

Date: _____

Today I Am Grateful For:

Todays Affirmation:

Find joy in your journey

Date: _____

Today I Am Grateful For:

Todays Affirmation:

Date: _____

Today I Am Grateful For:

Todays Affirmation:

Date: _____

Today I Am Grateful For:

Todays Affirmation:

Date: _____

Today I Am Grateful For:

Todays Affirmation:

Date: _____

Today I Am Grateful For:

Todays Affirmation:

Date: _____

Today I Am Grateful For:

Todays Affirmation:

Date: _____

Today I Am Grateful For:

Todays Affirmation:

Faith is seeing light with your heart

Date: _____

Today I Am Grateful For:

Todays Affirmation:

Date: _____

Today I Am Grateful For:

Todays Affirmation:

Date: _____

Today I Am Grateful For:

Todays Affirmation:

Date: _____

Today I Am Grateful For:

Todays Affirmation:

Date: _____

Today I Am Grateful For:

Todays Affirmation:

Date: _____

Today I Am Grateful For:

Todays Affirmation:

Date: _____

Today I Am Grateful For:

Todays Affirmation:

I can and I will
Watch me

Date: _____

Today I Am Grateful For:

Todays Affirmation:

Date: _____

Today I Am Grateful For:

Todays Affirmation:

Date: _____

Today I Am Grateful For:

Todays Affirmation:

Date: _____

Today I Am Grateful For:

Todays Affirmation:

Date: _____

Today I Am Grateful For:

Todays Affirmation:

Date: _____

Today I Am Grateful For:

Todays Affirmation:

Date: _____

Today I Am Grateful For:

Todays Affirmation:

You get what you work for
Not what you wish for

Date: _____

Today I Am Grateful For:

Todays Affirmation:

Date: _____

Today I Am Grateful For:

Todays Affirmation:

Date: _____

Today I Am Grateful For:

Todays Affirmation:

Date: _____

Today I Am Grateful For:

Todays Affirmation:

Date: _____

Today I Am Grateful For:

Todays Affirmation:

Date: _____

Today I Am Grateful For:

Todays Affirmation:

Date: _____

Today I Am Grateful For:

Todays Affirmation:

Life always offers a second chance
It's called tomorrow

Date: _____

Today I Am Grateful For:

Todays Affirmation:

Date: _____

Today I Am Grateful For:

Todays Affirmation:

Date: _____

Today I Am Grateful For:

Todays Affirmation:

Date: _____

Today I Am Grateful For:

Todays Affirmation:

Date: _____

Today I Am Grateful For:

Todays Affirmation:

Date: _____

Today I Am Grateful For:

Todays Affirmation:

Date: _____

Today I Am Grateful For:

Todays Affirmation:

Be fearless in what sets your soul on fire

Date: _____

Today I Am Grateful For:

Todays Affirmation:

Date: _____

Today I Am Grateful For:

Todays Affirmation:

Date: _____

Today I Am Grateful For:

Todays Affirmation:

Date: _____

Today I Am Grateful For:

Todays Affirmation:

Date: _____

Today I Am Grateful For:

Todays Affirmation:

Date: _____

Today I Am Grateful For:

Todays Affirmation:

Date: _____

Today I Am Grateful For:

Todays Affirmation:

Be Afraid And Do It Anyway

Date: _____

Today I Am Grateful For:

Todays Affirmation:

Date: _____

Today I Am Grateful For:

Todays Affirmation:

Date: _____

Today I Am Grateful For:

Todays Affirmation:

Printed in Great Britain
by Amazon